D1561115

DATE DUE

THIS LAND CALLED AMERICA: **NEBRASKA**

CREATIVE EDUCATION

Published by Creative Education
P.O. Box 227, Mankato, Minnesota 56002
Creative Education is an imprint of The Creative Company
www.thecreativecompany.us

Design by Blue Design (www.bluedes.com)
Art direction by Rita Marshall
Book production by The Design Lab
Printed in the United States of America

Photographs by Alamy (AGStockUSA, Inc., Danita Delimont, John Elk III,
Chuck Pefley, Tom Till, Worldwide Picture Library), Corbis (Patrick Bennett,
Bettmann, Historical Picture Archive, David Muench, Jim Richardson,
Arthur Rothstein), Getty Images (Stephen Ferry, Hulton Archive, Sarah
Leen/National Geographic, NBC Television, Edgar Samuel Paxson, Doug
Pensinger, Joel Sartore, Time & Life Pictures, Grey Villet/Time & Life
Pictures), iStockphoto (Uzi Tzur)

Library of Congress Cataloging-in-Publication Data
Hanel, Rachael.
Nebraska / by Rachael Hanel.
p. cm. — (This land called America)
Includes bibliographical references and index.
ISBN 978-1-58341-780-5
1. Nebraska—Juvenile literature. I. Title. II. Series.
F666.3.H36 2009
978.2—dc22   2008009509

First Edition
9 8 7 6 5 4 3 2 1

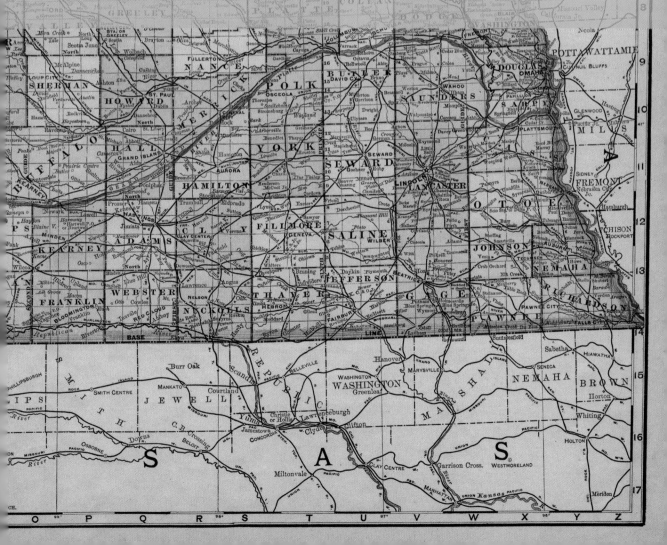

This Land Called America

NEBRASKA

Rachael Hanel

THIS LAND CALLED AMERICA

Nebraska

RACHAEL HANEL

THE OCTOBER SUN SHINES BRIGHTLY UPON NEBRASKA FIELDS. BUT A CHILL IN THE AIR SIGNALS THAT WINTER IS NOT FAR AWAY. THIS IS THE TIME OF YEAR WHEN FARMERS IN BIG TRACTORS DRIVE UP AND DOWN ROWS OF GOLDEN STALKS. THERE'S CORN AS FAR AS THE EYE CAN SEE. THE TRACTORS HARVEST THE KERNELS AND DROP THEM INTO LARGE TRUCKS. WHEN THE TRUCKS ARE FULL, DRIVERS TAKE THE CORN TO GRAIN ELEVATORS. THERE, THE CORN IS WEIGHED, AND FARMERS RECEIVE THEIR PAYMENTS. THIS CORN WILL BE PROCESSED AND END UP ON TABLES ACROSS THE UNITED STATES AND THROUGHOUT THE WORLD.

YEAR

1541 Explorer Francisco Vásquez de Coronado claims western America, including what is now Nebraska, for Spain.

EVENT

The Push West

Hundreds of years ago, Nebraska was a place of many landscapes. Tall prairie grass and leafy hardwood trees lined the Missouri River. Beavers and other animals roamed the lush valleys of the Missouri and Platte rivers. In the west, animals such as buffalo, pronghorn, and deer ranged in dry, short grass.

Many American Indian tribes called this land home. They lived in tight-knit communities, and some farmed the land. The Pawnee were the largest tribe. Other tribes included the Sioux, Oto, Omaha, Arapaho, and Ponca.

In the 16th century, Spain laid claim to much of western America, including Nebraska. Then, in the 1700s, Spanish and French explorers such as Pedro de Villasur and Pierre and Paul Mallet passed through Nebraska on their way west. The

YEAR
1739 French traders Paul and Pierre Mallet follow the Platte River to the Rocky Mountains.
EVENT

French claimed the land and set up a fur trade on the Missouri River. In 1803, President Thomas Jefferson bought the land from the French in the Louisiana Purchase.

The next year, Meriwether Lewis and William Clark scouted out the Louisiana Purchase territory for President Jefferson. In 1819, Major Stephen H. Long passed through Nebraska on his way to Wyoming. He believed the rugged land would be difficult to settle. He called it the "Great American Desert." In the 1840s, many pioneers traveling toward the Pacific Ocean passed through Nebraska on the Oregon Trail, but few stayed.

In 1854, the United States Congress created the Nebraska Territory. Pioneers slowly started to settle the area. They lived near rivers, where the land was easier to farm. Many settlers came from the eastern or southern U.S. By the late 1850s, much of eastern Nebraska was settled.

More people flooded the territory after the Homestead Act of 1862 was passed. This law gave people free land if they stayed for five years. Nebraska became America's 37th state on March 1, 1867. In parts of the state with few trees, pioneers cut large chunks of soil and grass, called sod, from the ground. They built their homes out of the sod.

Some American Indians fought against the pioneers. Gradually, the tribes were pushed off their traditional lands.

Meriwether Lewis and William Clark received help from Indian guides such as Sacagawea during their long journey west.

YEAR
1819   Major Stephen H. Long passes through Nebraska and names it the "Great American Desert."
EVENT

In the late 1800s, Nebraska farmers used large machines pulled by horses to harvest their wheat crop.

They were relocated to reservations, which were small sections of land set aside for them, or were forced into other territories. A few bands of Arapaho Indians lingered in far western Nebraska into the late 1800s. Few white people settled there because of the harsh landscape.

For a few years, life was good for Nebraska's pioneers. With hard work, they started successful farms. Ranchers from the southern U.S. thought the short grasses of western Nebraska were perfect for cattle grazing. The Union Pacific Railroad was finished in 1867 and ran through the entire state. Being close to the railroad helped ranchers and farmers buy and sell goods.

But soon, life took a turn for the worse. Grasshoppers infested the region throughout the 1870s. The insects destroyed crops and causesd many settlers to leave. The bitterly cold, snowy winter of 1880 and 1881 killed many cattle as well. Ranchers were left with nothing. Many quit and moved elsewhere.

Through the 1880s, the government offered free land again in hopes of luring settlers to Nebraska. As more railroads criss-crossed the state and new irrigation methods made it easier to supply water to crops in dry areas, pioneers started to return.

Railroad companies advertised land for sale in the West to get more people to move to Nebraska.

YEAR

1854   The Nebraska Territory is established by the U.S. Congress.

EVENT

- 10 -

MILLIONS OF ACRES

View on the Big Blue, between Camden and Crete, representing Valley and Rolling Prairie Land in Nebraska.

IOWA AND NEBRASKA LANDS

FOR SALE ON 10 YEARS CREDIT

BY THE

Burlington & Missouri River R.R.Co.

AT 6 PER CT. INTEREST AND LOW PRICES.

Only One-Seventh of Principal Due Annually, beginning Four Years after purchase.

20 PER CENT. DEDUCTED FROM 10 YEARS PRICE, FOR CASH.

LAND EXPLORING TICKETS SOLD

and Cost allowed in First Interest paid, on Land bought in 30 days from date of ticket.

Thus our Land Buyers ☞ GET A FREE PASS in the State where the Land bought is located.
These TERMS are BETTER at $5, than to pre-empt United States Land at $2.50 per Acre.
EXTRAORDINARY INDUCEMENTS on FREIGHT and PASSAGE are AFFORDED TO PURCHASERS and THEIR FAMILIES.

Address **GEO. S. HARRIS, LAND COMMISSIONER,**
or **T. H. LEAVITT, Ass't Land Comm'r, Burlington, Iowa.**

Or apply to

FREE ROOMS for buyers to board themselves are provided at Burlington and Lincoln.

COMMERCIAL ADVERTISER PRINTING HOUSE, BUFFALO, N. Y.

Great Plains State

Nebraska is located in the central part of the U.S. The Missouri River forms the state's entire eastern boundary and a small part of its northeastern border. Across the river lie Iowa and Missouri. Nebraska is bordered by South Dakota on the north. On the west, its neighbors are Wyoming and Colorado. To its south is Kansas.

Glaciers, or large sheets of moving ice, created Nebraska's landscape millions of years ago. A small sliver of eastern Nebraska is part of the Central Lowlands. This area is hilly and marked with sand and gravel that were left behind by glaciers.

Most of the rest of Nebraska is part of the Great Plains, a region which stretches from Texas to Montana. The western and northern portions of Nebraska are also known as the High Plains because they sit at a higher elevation than the rest of the Plains. The High Plains region is home to the highest point in Nebraska. Panorama Point, at 5,424 feet (1,653 m) above sea level, is located near the western town of Kimball.

In northwestern Nebraska, water and wind have worn away the earth's surface. This area is known as the Badlands. Smooth rock formations there are marked by swirls of earthy colors. The northwest is also home to large agate fossil beds, which contain the remains of ancient animals.

Nebraska's flat plains (opposite) are in sharp contrast to the rock outcroppings of Agate Fossil Beds National Monument (above).

G entle, grassy hills roll across north-central Nebraska. This area is good for cattle grazing. Throughout the central part of the state, a loose and yellowish-gray soil covers the ground. It is known as loess (*LESS*). The Loess Plains region contains many farms.

The Platte River, along with its north and south branches, runs through the state from west to east. It is wide and shallow. The branches meet in the town of North Platte. The Oto

*Cowboys drive herds of
cattle to Nebraska from
places farther north to
graze for the winter.*

Hundreds of small lakes are found in northern Nebraska. But the state's largest lakes are man-made. They were formed when engineers dammed rivers. The dams help control floods, and they provide power and water for crops. The most important crops are corn, wheat, and sorghum grain. Farmers and ranchers raise more cattle than any other animal. Nebraska is the third-biggest cattle-producing state in the U.S. Hogs are also an important farm animal in the state.

Nebraska sits atop important natural resources. Sand, gravel, and other rocks are extracted from the ground throughout the state. Clay is found in the southeast. Some oil and natural gas are also found in Nebraska.

Nebraska's climate is subject to extremes. That's because areas in the middle of a continent have more unpredictable weather than areas on the coasts. Some years, Nebraska will have heavy rains, while other years produce droughts. On average, annual rainfall in Nebraska is light. It ranges from fewer than 16 inches (41 cm) in the west to 34 inches (86 cm) in the southeast. Snowfall varies from 21 inches (53 cm) per year in the southeast to 45 inches (114 cm) per year in the northwest. In the summer, temperatures can climb above 90 °F (32 °C). But average January temperatures are around 30 °F (-1 °C).

When farmers do not have direct access to water, they use giant sprinklers to spray their fields.

YEAR

1872   The nation's first Arbor Day is celebrated in Nebraska.

EVENT

A Sense of Pride

MUCH LIKE THE AMERICAN INDIANS, NEBRASKA'S EARLIEST SETTLERS RECOGNIZED THE VALUE OF THE LAND'S RICH SOIL. PIONEERS TOOK ADVANTAGE OF THE FREE LAND OFFERED BY THE FEDERAL GOVERNMENT TO BUILD HOMES AND START FARMS. OTHERS WORKED ON THE RAILROAD. SOME RANCHERS MOVED FROM THE SOUTHERN U.S. IN SEARCH OF OPEN PASTURES FOR CATTLE AND SHEEP.

Although the state's early ranchers liked the wide-open spaces, other settlers missed the leafy trees of their homelands in Europe or on the East Coast. One settler, J. Sterling Morton, came to Nebraska from Michigan. He thought the state should have more trees. In 1872, he established the first Arbor Day. More than one million trees were planted on that one day. Arbor Day became a public holiday in 1885.

Nebraska's landscape and heritage inspired early 20th-century author Willa Cather. Cather was born in Virginia, but

Early settlers built their homes near rivers (opposite), and farmers plowed their fields with the help of horses well into the 1900s (above).

YEAR
1877

EVENT

Sioux chief Crazy Horse surrenders to the U.S. Army in Nebraska, and his tribe is forced onto a reservation.

Although Willa Cather later moved out east, much of her writing remained rooted in Nebraska.

when she was 10 years old, she moved with her family to Red Cloud, Nebraska. She used her adopted state as the backdrop for many of her novels. Cather's novel, *One of Ours,* won the famous Pulitzer Prize. It is the story of a Nebraska farm boy who fights in World War I. Another of her books, *O Pioneers!,* tells the story of life on the Nebraska frontier.

Another famous person to call Nebraska home was comedian and talk-show host Johnny Carson. Although Carson was born in Iowa, his family moved to Norfolk, Nebraska, when he was a child. He graduated from the University of Nebraska in 1949. Two years later, Carson left the state to begin his career in television. He was the host of *The Tonight Show* for 30 years.

Entertainer Johnny Carson hosted The Tonight Show *from 1962 until 1992, when he retired.*

YEAR

1919   Three people are killed by gunfire when tensions between whites and African Americans flare in Omaha.

EVENT

- *20* -

'62-'63

'63-'64

'65-'66

'64-'65

'66-'67

'67-'68

'68-'69

'69-'70

'70-'71

'73-'74

'71-'72

'72-'73

'74-'75

'77-'78

The people of Nebraska contribute to the state's economy in many ways. One of the state's most important industries is agriculture. More than 48,000 farms dot Nebraska's landscape. Farms support many other businesses as well. Workers are needed to make and sell tractors. Many people work in factories that process grain and package meat. Products made from Nebraska's grain and meat eventually go to grocery stores and restaurants across the U.S.

Nebraska's agricultural industry is also responsible for cutting-edge ethanol production. Ethanol is a fuel that provides an alternative to gasoline and oil. It is produced from corn. As of 2008, Nebraska ranked second among U.S. states in ethanol production.

The insurance business is also an important one in Nebraska. Mutual of Omaha is the state's largest firm. It sponsored a popular TV show, *Mutual of Omaha's Wild Kingdom*, from 1963 to 1988.

After corn is harvested (opposite), it is taken to a grain elevator (above) to be weighed and either stored or shipped.

YEAR
1937   Nebraska's legislature holds its first session to make the state's laws.
EVENT

Nebraska students

Industry, business, and natural resources continue to attract people to Nebraska. So do the state's clean air and blue skies. The state always ranks high in health quality. In Nebraska, there are only 22.3 persons per square mile (2.6 sq km). This makes Nebraska one of the least densely populated states in the country. But each year, the population of Nebraska steadily grows. The largest towns are found along the state's many rivers.

Most of the people in Nebraska are white. People of Hispanic origin, mostly from Mexico, make up more than seven percent of the population. Asian Americans, African Americans, and American Indians make up a small percentage of the total population.

Students (above) at Nebraska's universities cheer for their sports teams and are proud to live in a state with impressive cities such as Omaha (opposite).

WOODMEN

ConAgra

YEAR
1982   A new law bars Nebraska farmers from selling their land to large companies.
EVENT

A Sense of Community

NEBRASKA HAS THE SMALLEST STATE GOVERNMENT IN THE COUNTRY. ITS UNICAMERAL (ONE-CHAMBER) SYSTEM INCLUDES ONLY A SENATE OF 49 SENATORS, OR MEMBERS. ALL OTHER STATES HAVE BICAMERAL (TWO-CHAMBER) GOVERMENTS WITH BOTH A HOUSE OF REPRESENTATIVES AND A SENATE. BECAUSE OF ITS LESS-COMPLICATED SYSTEM, NEBRASKA'S GOVERNMENT IS ABLE TO WORK MORE EFFICIENTLY.

Another of Nebraska's distinctions is that it is home to the famous drink mix Kool-Aid. Kool-Aid was invented by chemist Edwin Perkins. He found a way to make a powder that would mix with water to form a fruity, colorful drink. A museum in Hastings holds a collection devoted to Kool-Aid, the official soft drink of Nebraska.

The Oregon Trail, which helped people get to the West Coast in the 1800s, went past Chimney Rock.

Nebraska also boasts many natural attractions. Chimney Rock is the most famous monument in Nebraska. It was chosen to be on the back of Nebraska's state quarter in 2006. Located in far western Nebraska, this narrow column of rock rises 325 feet (99 m) from its base. It was carved by thousands of years of wind and rain. The rock was given the name "Chimney Rock" because many pioneers on the Oregon Trail thought it looked like a chimney. Today, visitors can hike around Chimney Rock, but they cannot climb it because it is made out of soft sandstone that is easily worn away.

The state capitol in Lincoln was the first in the U.S. to use an office tower as part of the design.

Every spring, tourists in Nebraska are treated to another amazing sight as thousands of sandhill cranes gather at the Platte River. The river is an important stop for the cranes

YEAR
2004   University of Nebraska English professor Ted Kooser is selected as U.S. poet laureate.
EVENT

- 27 -

Omaha's Offutt Air Force Base, named for a local man who was killed in World War I, trains pilots to fly.

as they fly north to Canada from Texas, New Mexico, and Mexico. On the Platte, they rest and eat before continuing their long journey. When they leave, the high-pitched trilling of thousands of birds fills the air.

Because of its location, Nebraska served an important military role after World War II. The nation's Strategic Air Command (SAC) was located at Offutt Air Force Base south of Omaha. Military leaders wanted the SAC to be headquartered in America's heartland. They believed that the likelihood of an attack by foreign enemies was lower inland. The SAC (which became the unified Strategic Command in 1992) controls the country's nuclear weapons and forces.

One thing that endures in Nebraska is a love of sports, even though the state does not have any professional sports teams. Instead, people get excited about the College Baseball World Series, which is held every year in Omaha. In the fall, college football is king. The University of Nebraska Cornhuskers compete in the Big 12 Conference and were five-time national champions by the 2000s. On game day, spectators wear the school colors of red and white to support the team.

In addition to taking pride in their college teams, Nebraskans take pride in their families and communities. In 1982, voters passed a constitutional amendment banning corporations

Nebraska Cornhuskers football has had one of the proudest programs in the nation for more than 100 years.

YEAR

2005   Former Nebraska governor Mike Johanns is appointed as U.S. secretary of agriculture.

EVENT

QUICK FACTS

Population: 1,774,571

Largest city: Omaha (pop. 424,482)

Capital: Lincoln

Entered the union: March 1, 1867

Nickname: Cornhusker State

State flower: goldenrod

State bird: western meadowlark

Size: 77,354 sq mi (200,346 sq km)—16th-biggest in U.S.

Major industries: farming, ranching, meat packing, insurance

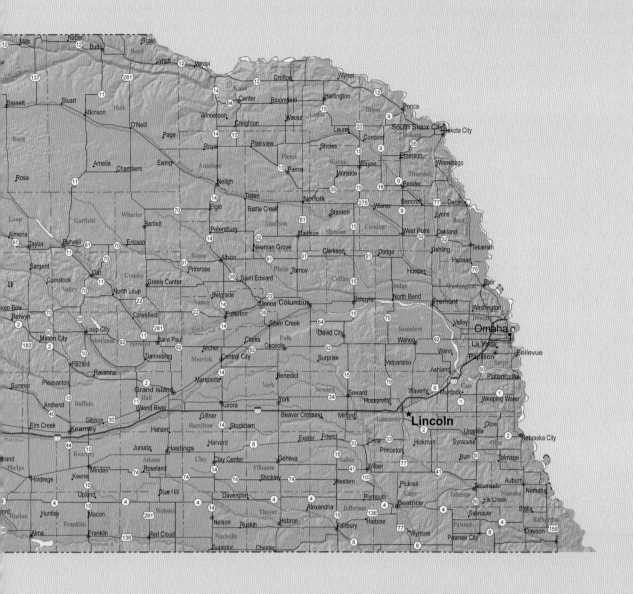

without Nebraska ties from buying farms. Voters wanted to make sure that the state's farms would always be owned by the people who live and work in Nebraska.

As the U.S. population grows, so does the demand for food and alternative energy sources, such as ethanol. With its endless fields and hard-working people, "The Cornhusker State" is ready to meet those demands. The state will remain an important source of corn for Americans' tables and cars far into the future.

BIBLIOGRAPHY

Baltensperger, Bradley H. *Nebraska: A Geography.* Boulder, Colo.: Westview Press, 1985.

Federal Writers' Project of the Works Progress Administration for the State of Nebraska. *Nebraska: Guide to the Cornhusker State.* Lincoln, Neb.: University of Nebraska Press, 1979.

Olson, James C., and Ronald C. Naugle. *History of Nebraska.* Lincoln, Neb.: University of Nebraska Press, 1997.

U.S. Census Bureau. "Nebraska." U.S. Census Bureau: State and County QuickFacts. http://quickfacts.census.gov/qfd/states/31000.html.

Worldmark Encyclopedia of the States. Vol. 2. Detroit: Thomson Gale, 2007.

INDEX